PINK FLOYD FOR UKULELE

Cover photo © Photofest

T0057623

ISBN 978-1-4803-9286-1

HAL•LEONARD®
CORPORATION
7777 W. BLUEMOUND RD. P.O. BOX 13819 MILWAUKEE, WI 53213

Visit Hal Leonard Online at
www.halleonard.com

Another Brick in the Wall, Part 2

Words and Music by Roger Waters

Teach - er, leave __ them __ kids a - lone. __
Teach - er, leave __ us __ kids a - lone. __

Hey, teach - er! Leave them kids a - lone! ____
Hey, teach - er! Leave us kids a - lone! ____

Chorus

All in all, __ it's just an - oth - er brick in the
All in all, __ you're just an - oth - er brick in the

wall.
wall.

All in all, __ you're just an -

- oth - er brick in the wall.

Brain Damage

Words and Music by Roger Waters

1. The lu - na - tic _____ is on the grass. _____
2. *See additional lyrics*

The lu - na - tic _____ is on the grass. _____

Re - mem - ber - ing games and dai - sy chains _____ and laughs. _____

1. Got to keep _____ the loon - ies on _____ the path. _____

2. ev - 'ry day _____ the pa - per - boy _____ brings more.

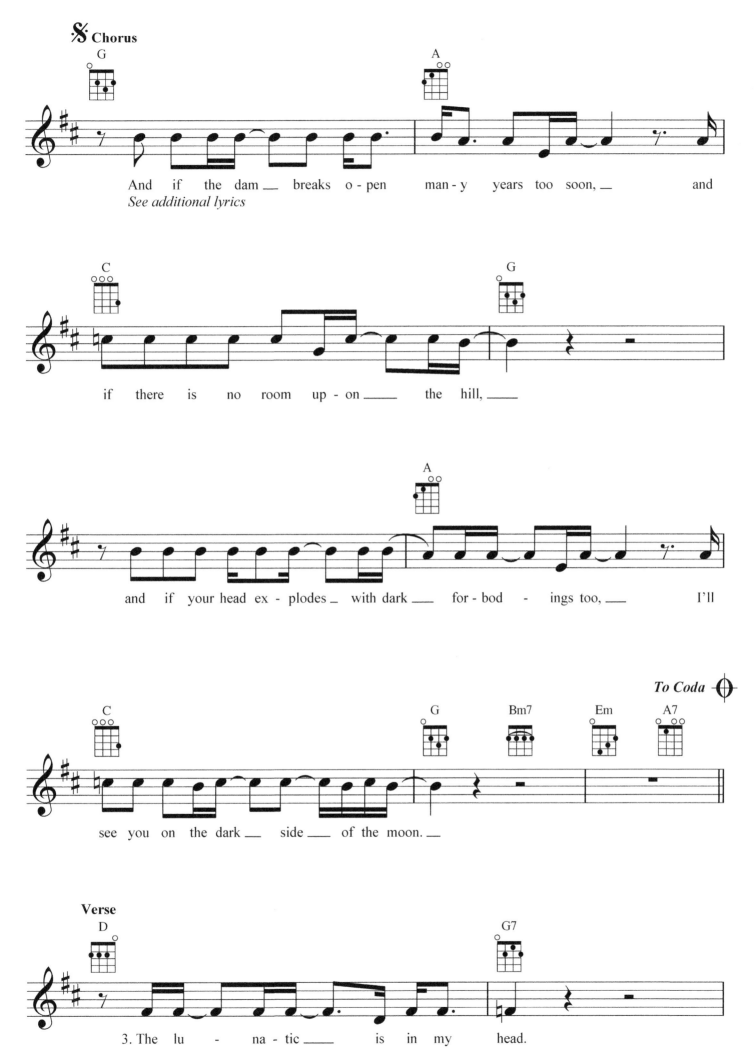

The lu - na - tic _____ is in my head.

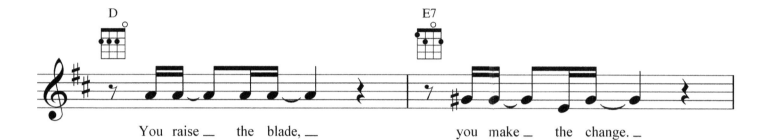

You raise _ the blade, _ you make _ the change. _

You re - ar - range _ me 'til I'm sane. ___

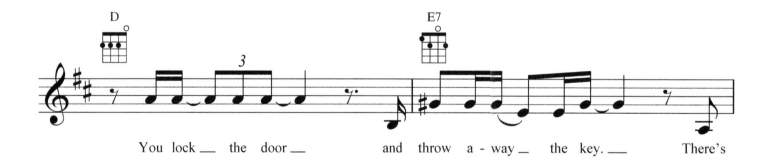

You lock _ the door _ and throw a - way _ the key. _ There's

D.S. al Coda

some - one in my head, but it's not me.

6

Outro-Verse

(Spoken:) I can't think of anything to say, I mean, so...   *(laughs)*

I think it's numbness.   *(laughs)*

Additional Lyrics

2. The lunatic is in the hall.
     The lunatics are in my hall.
     The paper holds their folded faces to the floor,
     And ev'ry day the paperboy brings more.

Chorus: And if the cloud bursts, thunder in your ear,
           You shout and no one seems to hear.
           And if the band you're in starts playing diff'rent tunes,
           I'll see you on the dark side of the moon.

Breathe

Words by Roger Waters
Music by Roger Waters, David Gilmour and Rick Wright

All you touch _ and all _ you see is all your life _ will ev - er be.

Verse

2. Run, _ rab - bit, run. _____ Dig that hole, ____ get ___ the sun. _

_____ When _ at last ___ your work _ is done, _

don't sit down; _ it's time ___ to dig ____ an - oth - er one.

Long you live ___ and high ___ you fly, but on - ly if _____ you ride ___ the tide.

Bal - anced on ____ the big - gest wave, race to - wards _ an ear - ly grave.

Green Is the Colour

Words and Music by Roger Waters

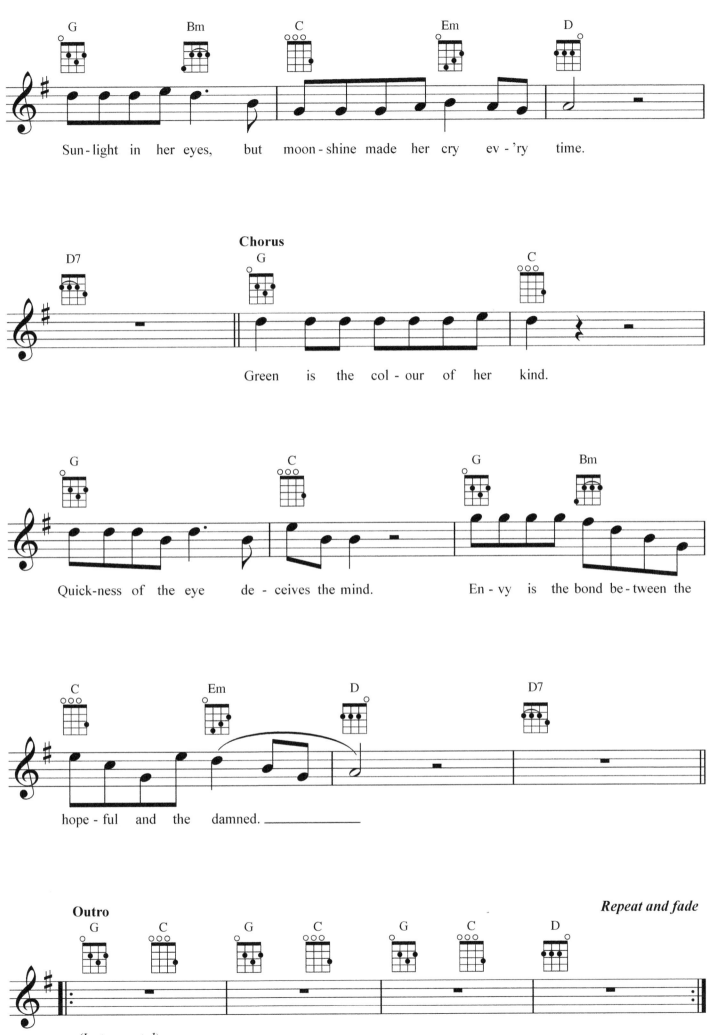

Have a Cigar

Words and Music by Roger Waters

Hey You

Words and Music by Roger Waters

And the worms ate in-to his brain.

Verse

3. Hey you! Out there on the road, al-ways

do-ing what you're told, can you help me? Hey you! Out

there be-yond the wall, break-ing bot-tles in the hall, can you help me?

Chorus

Hey you! Don't tell me there's no hope at all. ____

To - geth - er we stand, di - vid - ed we fall. ___

Let chord ring.

Comfortably Numb

Words and Music by Roger Waters and David Gilmour

17

Just the ba - sic facts. __ Can you show me where __ it hurts?
go - ing for __ the show. __ Come on, it's time __ to go.

Pre-Chorus

There is __ no pain; __ you are __ re - ced - ing.

A dis - tant ship's __ smoke on __ the ho - ri - zon.

You are on - ly com - ing through __ in waves. __ Your

lips move, __ but I can't hear __ what you're say - ing.
When
When

Chorus

I was a child, I __ had a fe - ver.
I was a child, I __ caught a fleet - ing glimpse __

My

Money

Words and Music by Roger Waters

Chorus

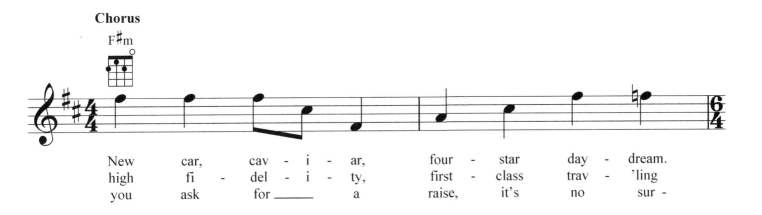

New   car,   cav -   i -   ar,   four -   star   day -   dream.
high   fi -   del -   i -   ty,   first -   class   trav -   'ling
you   ask   for _____   a   raise,   it's   no   sur -

1., 2.

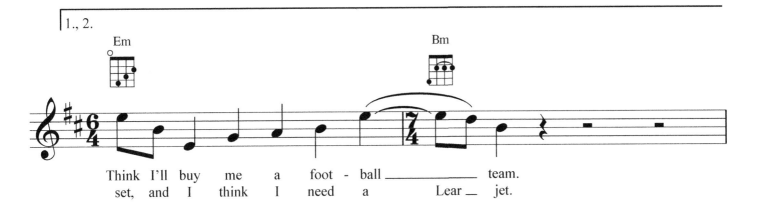

Think   I'll   buy   me   a   foot -   ball _____   team.
set,   and   I   think   I   need   a   Lear _   jet.

3.

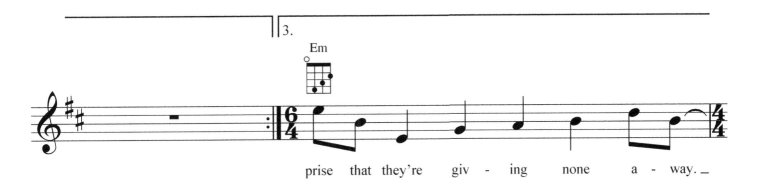

prise   that   they're   giv -   ing   none   a -   way._

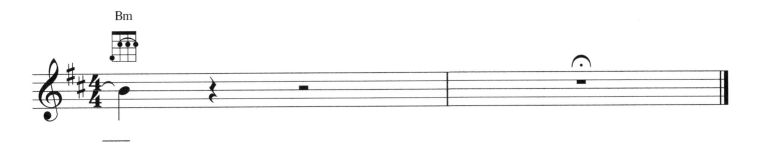

Mother

Words and Music by Roger Waters

1. Moth-er, do you think they'll drop __ the bomb?
2. Moth-er, should I run for pres - i - dent?
3. Moth-er, do you think she's good __ e - nough

(3.) for me?

Moth - er, do you think they'll like ___ this song?
Moth - er, should I trust the gov - ern - ment?
Moth - er, do you think she's dan - ger - ous

(3.) to me?

Moth - er, do you think they'll try ___ to break ___ my balls?
Moth - er, will they put me in ___ the fir - ing line?
Moth - er, will she tear your lit - tle boy ___ a - part?

Ooh, ah, Moth - er, should I build the wall? _
Ooh, ah, is it just a waste of time? _
Ooh, ah, Moth - er, will she break my heart? _

1.

2., 3.

Chorus

Hush now, ba - by, ba - by, don't you cry.
Hush now, ba - by, ba - by, don't you cry.

Ma - ma's gon - na make all of your night - mares come true.
Ma - ma's gon - na check out all your girl - friends for you.

Ma - ma's gon - na put all of her fears in - to you.
Ma - ma won't let an - y - one dirt - y get through.

Ma - ma's gon - na keep you right here un - der her wing. She
Ma - ma's gon - na wait up un - til you get in.

won't let you fly, but she might let you sing.
Ma - ma will al - ways find out where you've been.

Ma - ma's gon - na keep ba - by co - zy and warm.
Ma - ma's gon - na keep ba - by health - y and clean.

Ooh, babe, ___ ooh, babe, ___
Ooh, babe, ___ ooh, babe, ___

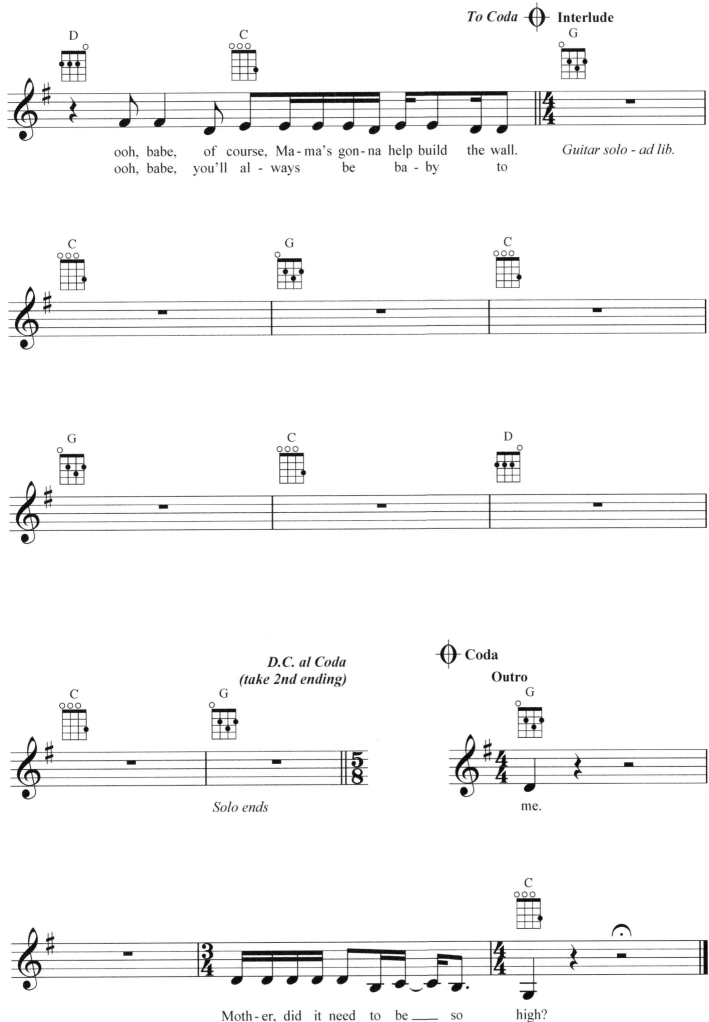

To Coda ⊕ **Interlude**

ooh, babe, of course, Ma-ma's gon-na help build the wall. *Guitar solo - ad lib.*
ooh, babe, you'll al-ways be ba-by to

D.C. al Coda
(take 2nd ending)

Solo ends

⊕ **Coda**

Outro

me.

Moth-er, did it need to be ___ so high?

Pigs on the Wing
(Part 1)

Words and Music by Roger Waters

First note

Moderately fast

Verse

If you did-n't care what hap-pened to me and I did-n't care for you, we would zig - zag our way through the

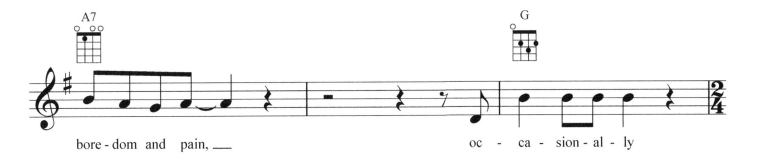

bore - dom and pain, ___

oc - ca - sion - al - ly

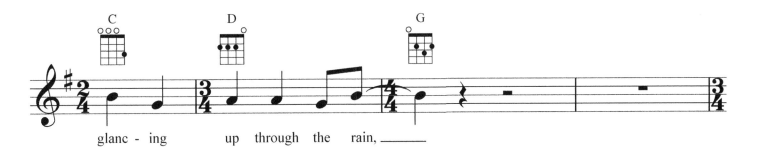

glanc - ing   up through the rain, _____

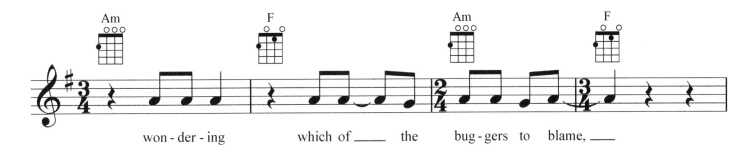

won - der - ing   which of ___ the   bug - gers to blame, ___

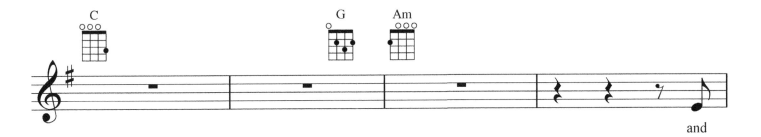

and

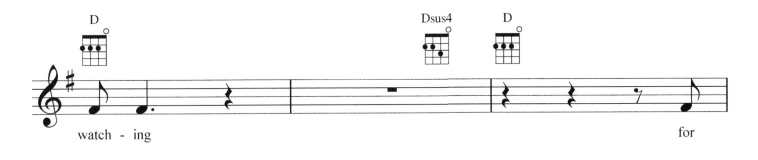

watch - ing   for

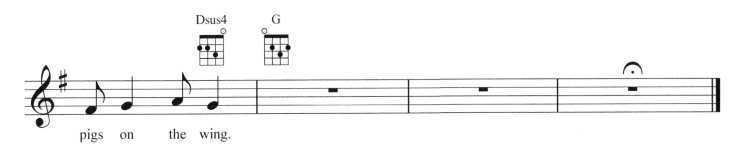

pigs   on   the wing.

Time

Words and Music by Roger Waters, Nicholas Mason, David Gilmour and Rick Wright

Us and Them

Words by Roger Waters
Music by Roger Waters and Rick Wright

Chorus

1. "For - ward," he cried ___ from the rear, and the front rank
(2., 3.) *See additional lyrics*

died. ___ The gen - 'ral sat, ___ and the

lines on the map moved from side ___ to ___

To Coda

1. side.

2. side." *D.C. al Coda*

Coda died.

Additional Lyrics

2. Black and blue,
   And who knows which is which and who is who.
   Up and down,
   And in the end it's only 'round and 'round and 'round.

Chorus: "Haven't you heard it's a battle of words?"
   The poster bearer cried.
   "Listen, son," said the man with the gun,
   "There's room for you inside."

3. Down and out,
   It can't be helped, but there's a lot of it about.
   With, without,
   And who'll deny that's what the fighting's all about?

Chorus: Out of the way; it's a busy day.
   I've got things on my mind.
   For want of the price of tea and a slice,
   The old man died.

Welcome to the Machine

Words and Music by Roger Waters

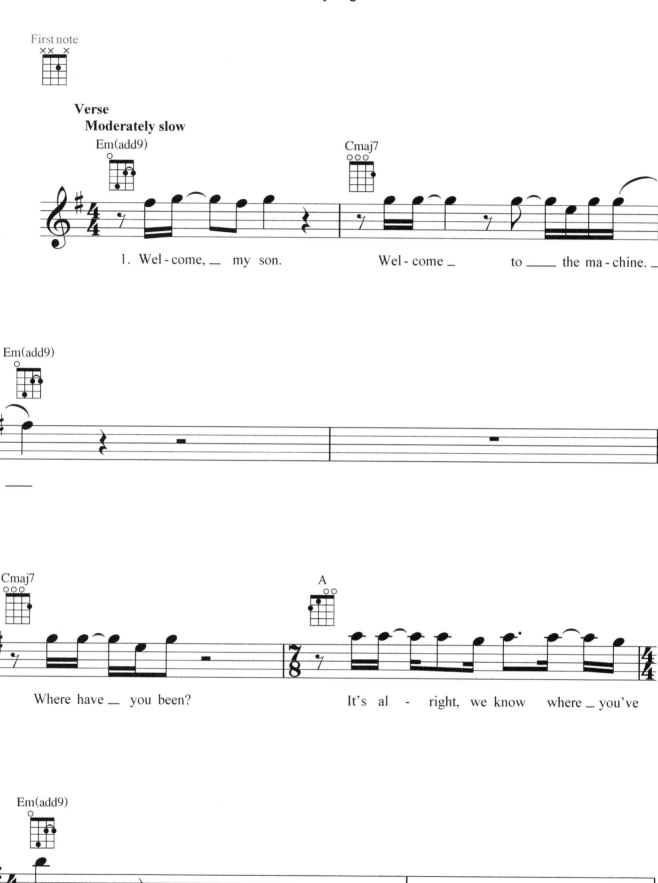

1. Wel-come, — my son. Wel-come — to — the ma-chine.

Where have — you been? It's al - right, we know where — you've

been.

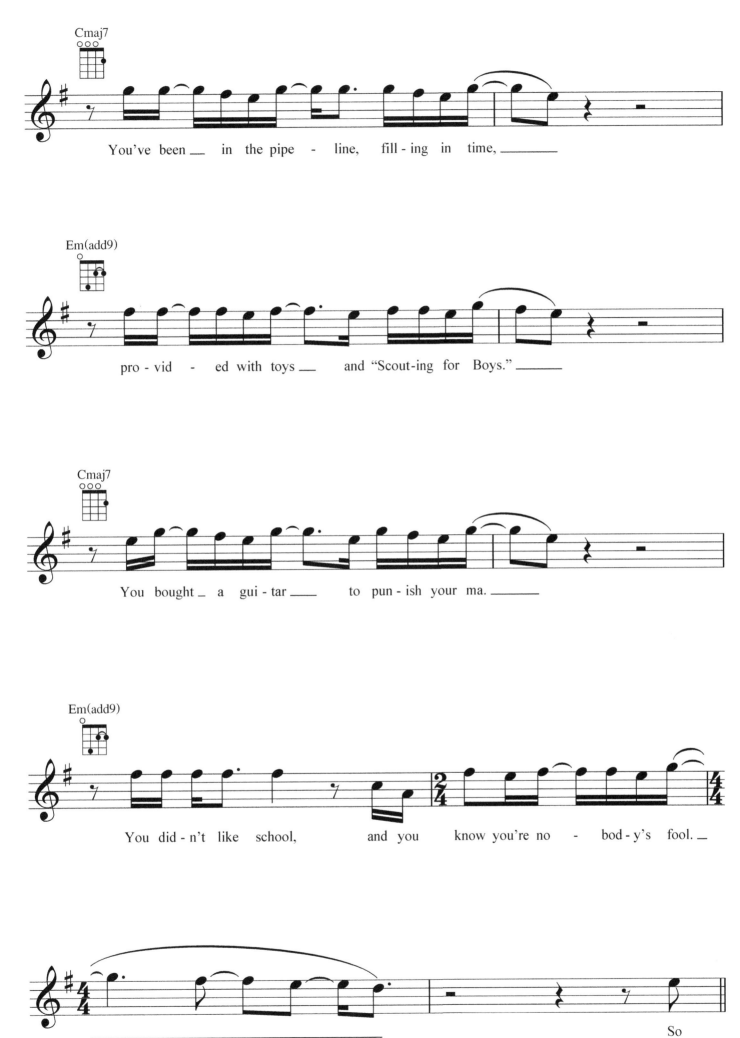

Cmaj7

You've been ___ in the pipe - line, fill - ing in time, _____

Em(add9)

pro - vid - ed with toys ___ and "Scout-ing for Boys." _____

Cmaj7

You bought ___ a gui - tar ___ to pun - ish your ma. _____

Em(add9)

You did - n't like school, and you know you're no - bod - y's fool. ___

So

Chorus

Cmaj7

wel - come _____ to ____ the ma - chine. __

Em(add9)

Verse

Em(add9)   Cmaj7

2. Wel - come, __ my son.   Wel - come _____ to ____ the ma - chine. __

Em(add9)

C   A

What did ____ you dream?   It's al - right, we told you what __ to

Em(add9)

dream. _____

Young Lust

Words and Music by Roger Waters and David Gilmour

- an.

Ooh, _____

_____ I need a dirt - y girl. ___

Verse

Fine

2. Will some wom - an in this des - ert land _____

make me feel ___ like a real ___ man? ___

Take this rock and roll ___ ref - u - gee, ___

D.S. al Fine

ooh, babe, set me free. ___

Wish You Were Here

Words and Music by Roger Waters and David Gilmour

Interlude

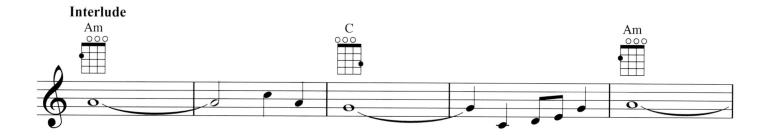

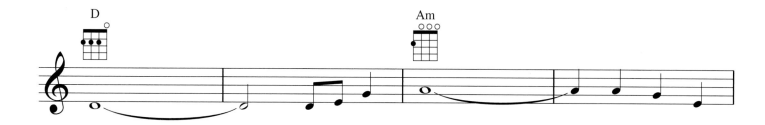

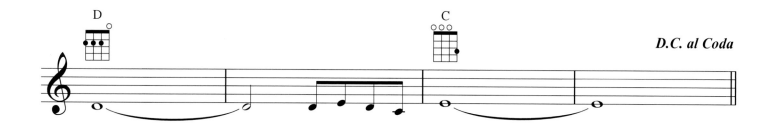

D.C. al Coda

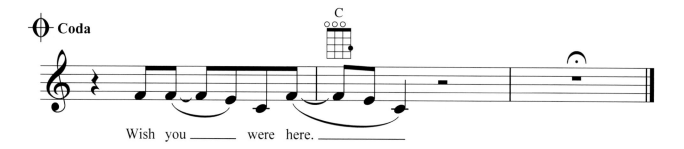

Wish you _____ were here. _____

Additional Lyrics

2. How I wish, how I wish you were here.
   We're just two lost souls swimming in a fish bowl year after year.
   Running over the same old ground, what have we found?
   The same old fears. Wish you were here.